100 WAYS to Say I Love You Mother

Copyright © James Watson

Publisher Checkmate Inc.
All rights reserved. No part of this book may be reproduced
In any manner whatsoever, without written permission from
the publisher.
Library of congress catalog number:
97-91653
ISNB; 0-9641356-3-9
Manufactured in the United States of America.
First printing March of 1997: second print and revision Jan 2012.
Print.

DEDICATION

This book is dedicated to my

Mother, Jessie Watson who

Has raised two generations of

Kids, and to my daughter,

Shanika who has just begun

To experience the Motherhood

Of my three grandkids Torrigue,

Torrincia and Michael.

It is dedicated to all

The caring and loving

Women who are Mothers

And to all future Mothers of

The world.

EDITOR'S COMMENTS

After reading this book Linda Williams my Managing Editor said, this book Took her "Love" and "Appreciation" for her Mother to a new and Higher level.

I hope you come to feel The same.

THANK YOU

I would like to thank all my

Friends for their support and

Encouragement, During the

Writing of this book,

Especially Vida Addison and

Charles Ferguson. For if it wasn't for them

Purchasing my first book

"50 Ways to Say I Love You."

I don't believe I would have

had the Determination, Inspiration

and courage to write this book.

Thank you all,
James Watson (Author)

TABLE OF CONTENT

1. Gifts
2. Character
3. Influence of the environment
4. Protector
5. Devotion
6. Comforter
7. Your Smile
8. Sacrificing
9. Respecting
10. Separating
11. Friendship
12. Motherly Love
13. Inspiration
14. Motivation
15. Togetherness
16. Obligations
17. Career
18. Unconditional Love
19. Priceless Love
20. Inner Beauty
21. Ambassadress
22. Caring
23. One of a Kind
24. Remembering
25. Heir Loom
26. Importance of Friendship
27. Sharing Experience
28. Number One Mom
29. I owe you my Life
30. Confidant
31. Generous Love

TABLE OF CONTENT

32. Managing Money
33. Mother Clichés
34. Seed Sowing
35. A Happy Face
36. Motherly Traits
37. Mistakes
38. Hall of Fame
39. Happiness in Life
40. Teacher
41. Mother's famous Quotes
42. Commitment
43. The Value of Education
44. Today's Mothers
45. No Bad Habits
46. Mother's Ten Golden Rules
47. Honesty and Love
48. Talked About
49. Questions in Life
50. Wisdom of Money
51. Her Presence
52. Being There
53. Life
54. Mannerism
55. Many Facet of Love
56. Greatest Mom
57. Making a Difference
58. Blessing the Food
59. through my Eyes
60. Always Praising
61. Cuddling Arms
62. Right and Wrong

TABLE OF CONTENT

63. Honor Thy Mother
64. Loves a Noun
65. Loves invisible Shield
66. The Rose
67. The Effects of Love
68. Love (a precious award)
69. Holiday and Days
70. Mother's Autobiography
71. A wealth of Love
72. Glowing
73. Wrong Perception of Love
74. Thoughts That Count
75. A continuous Flow of Love
76. The need for each other
77. The journey of Life
78. Description of a Mother
79. Forgiveness of a Mother
80. Ingredients of Love
81. Mansion
82. Nicknames
83. Different Languages
84. Intuitive Powers
85. Twins
86. Faith
87. Miracles
88. Say It with Love
89. Touch by an Angel
90. Change
91. Saint
92. Worrying
93. Timeless Commitment of Love
94. Love
95. Love is Given Freely
96. Immeasurable Love
97. True Meaning of Love
98. Happiness
99. Love (Internally and Eternally)
100. A Million Times

GIFTS

As you received this

Mother's Day gift from me

It's only a small token,

Compared to the many gifts

You have given me.

So, please accept this gift

From me with all my love

On this Mother's Day.

I LOVE YOU

Character

*I never heard you spoke
Harshly of others, I never
Heard you use profanity in
Anyway, I never heard you
speak in a loud tone, I
never heard you argue with
anyone, now I know there
are angels on this earth.*

I LOVE YOU

INFLUENCE OF THE ENVIRONMENT

They say we are a product

Of our environment. The

Other day I was investing

Money in something, when

Something took hold of me

And made me realize That I

had acquired the Knowledge

and smarts from you, Mother. Thanks A million, Mother,
for you are truly worth

A million dollars.

I LOVE YOU

PROTECTOR

The journey of life begins

With one's mother as

Someone who comfort

You, nurture you,

Protects you, educates you,

And ultimately provides

You with the wisdom to

Stand on your own.

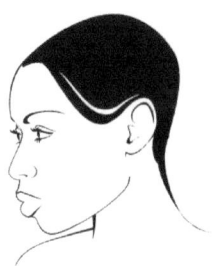

I LOVE YOU

DEVOTION

Thanks for the endless

Hours of devotion.

Thanks for the endless

Hours of patience, Thanks

For the endless

Hours of encouragement,

For you truly gave up

Your time so that I could

Have a successful life.

Happy Mother's Day

I LOVE YOU

COMFORTER

You kiss the pain away

When it hurt the most then

Wipe the tears away and

Said the hurting would soon

Go away, and you were so

right. So it was the little

Things you did that made a

Big difference in my life,

Mother.

Happy Mother's Day

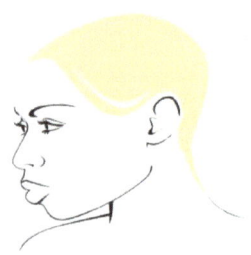

I LOVE YOU

YOUR SMILE

Your smile brought so

Much happiness in times of

Despair. Your smile took

Away the sorrow that was

In the air, your smile made

It right when wrong was

There, your smile is like a

Rose, you received not

Knowing who, what, or why

But grateful for the caring thought.

I LOVE YOU

SACRIFICING

Being an adult makes you

Realize all the sacrifices your

Mother made so that you could

Have some of the materialist things

That makes you happy. Thanks Mom

For not buying that expensive

Dress that you knew would look

So good on you. Thanks you for

not attending the show that was

so important to you: for sacrifices

are one of the main ingredients of

being a good a Mother.

I LOVE YOU

RESPECTING

As I reflect on my first date you

Said always treat her like you

Would treat your Mother.

1. Always open doors
2. Be a gentleman at all times
3. Never hit a lady

Thanks to you "Mom" I have a

Beautiful wife, who is also a

precious Mother. For young

ladies grow up to be Mothers.

Thanks Mom for your

Motherly wit.

I LOVE YOU

SEPARATING

First we were inseparable,

Fortunately for me, secondly

You carried me in your arms,

How lucky for me, thirdly you

Held on to my hand so I knew

To stay by your side, that was

Good for me, fortunately for me you

Knew when to let go of my hand,

While still keeping your eyes on me,

Guidance was a part of the love that

you gave to me.

Happy Mother's Day

I LOVE YOU

FRIENDSHIP

When my friends said that

I couldn't do it, you were

There to say "I could."

Thanks Mom for your undying

Support and being the best friend

In the world.

Friends Always!

I LOVE YOU

MOTHERLY LOVE

Motherly love is one of a

Kind, special and unique. I

wish I could gift wrap your

motherly love for everyone

on this Mother's Day.

I know I could never say thank you

Enough but anyway,

Happy Mother's Day.

I LOVE YOU

INSPIRATION

Although we didn't have

All the necessities growing

Up, you taught us to be

Thankful for what we had,

And inspired in us that

Tomorrow will be a better

And brighter day with lots

of sunshine. Thanks for

the inspiration during the stormy

weather and rough times.

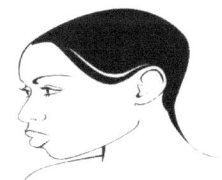

I LOVE YOU

MOTIVATION

You always said the most

Important role model is

self. Plan your work and

work your plan and good

things will come your way

but always believe in GOD and self

first.

Thanks Mom for being my

Mentor as well as my number

One motivator.

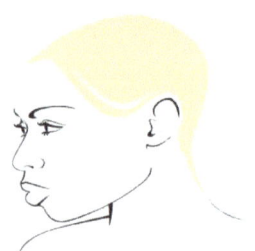

I LOVE YOU

TOGETHERNESS

It's not the quantity of time

We spent together but the

Quality of time that we

Spent together <u>Cliché</u>.

Thank God you were smart

Enough to know that both

Quality and quantity were

Important.

MAMMA

I LOVE YOU

OBLIGATIONS

You took me to the basketball

Games, you took me to the

Football games, you took me

To dance lessons, you took me

To gymnastic classes; you

Believed in me in every way;

When I brought the Gold metal

Home; when I brought the football

Championship home; I owe it all to you, Mom.

Thanks-this one is for you.

I LOVE YOU

CAREER

There were times when I

Thought about moving away

From you for personal Opportunities or career

Advancement. But I thought

About it diligently, then came to

The conclusion, what if you (Mom) Disrupted

my young adolescent life For those same

things supra Would I be where I am today?

so I decided to stay close to you to help you

as you grow old gracefully in your time of need.

I will develop my career and opportunities

around you instead of without you.

I LOVE YOU

UNCONDITIONAL LOVE

MOM

Unconditional Love is what

You preach and practice the most,

Always say you are sorry, when

You do something wrong, always be

Thankful, grateful, and truthful.

Never, never, ever put a price on love.

Always give 100% of yourself in

Whatever you're doing in life.

I LOVE YOU

PRICELESS LOVE

For all the wealth I own.

For all the diamonds I can

Buy.

For all the pearls I can store.

For all the Gold I can find.

I thank God for you

For I would give all my wealth

Away today for you, Mom.

Your Love is Priceless!

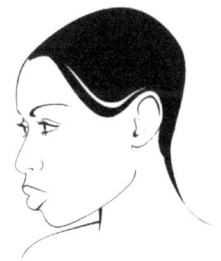

I LOVE YOU

INNER BEAUTY

Your hair is a little gray now.

Your face is a little wrinkled

Your walk is a little slower

But you are by far still the best

Mom in the world to me.

Beauty is only skin deep and

That inner beauty is more

Important and everlasting.

Thank for that lesson in life.

I LOVE YOU

AMBASSADRESS

If I had the power to

Appoint you as world

Ambassadress

I would do so. Surely you

Exhibit in your life, peace, love,

Goodwill, and kindness toward

everyone to win a Nobel Peace prize.

MOTHER

I LOVE YOU

CARING

Thanks Mom for caring for

me all those years.

Thanks Mom for teaching me

to care for others.

For if I could use one word

To describe you, it would be

CARING.

Happy Mother's Day

I LOVE YOU

ONE OF A KIND

You may have many friends

You may have a great wife

You may have an exceptionally

Good father.

You may have a successful

Career.

But there is nothing like a

Wonderful mother.

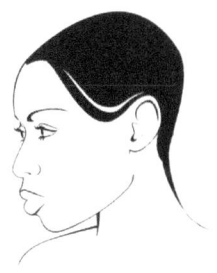

I LOVE YOU

REMEMBERING

I know some people only

Remember their mothers only

On Mother's Day.

I'm glad I remember you

Every day and think about you

every moment of the day.

I often think about the good

Times you gave me.

I hope and pray I have given

you some good times in return.

Happy Mother's Day.

I LOVE YOU

HEIR LOOM

In our society, it's usually

Mothers who have handed down

Heirlooms. I will always

Remember the gift you gave me

On my wedding day and you

Said, "this was given to me by

Your grandmother, so I am now

Giving it to you today, so that you will

Give it to your daughter. Those special

Moments I will cherish forever. Thank You

NANNA and Thank you Mom

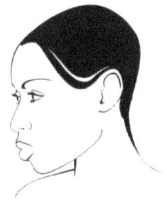

I LOVE YOU

IMPORTANCE OF FRIENDSHIP

You pointed out to me the importance of developing good friendships, so that I would never be lonely in life. And as I lived my life I emphasize to those I meet in everyday living the importance of having someone they can call a friend. And as I go about spreading your message of Friendship, I thank you for being my Mother as well as my friend.

I LOVE YOU

SHARING EXPERIENCES

Mom

As I reflect on the memories of my childhood, the good and the bad, you were always there to share those experiences with me. First I would like to thank you for being there and secondly thanks for sharing your love and life experiences with me.

I love you.

NUMBER ONE MOM

For all the things you did

for me in my,

adolescence and adult life,

You will always be

unquestionable the number

one Mom in my life

always.

Happy Mother's Day

I LOVE YOU

I OWE YOU MY LIFE

There is an old adage when

Someone saves your life. You

Always owe that person your

Life. Well you save my life

Many times by giving me the

Right advice at the right time.

So I guess I owe you more than

My life.

Happy Mother's Day.

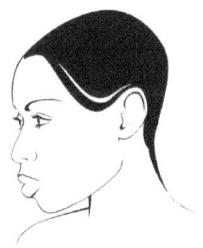

I LOVE YOU

CONFIDANT

When I was ten years old you sat

Me down on the living room sofa

And said, you had something

important to tell me. I thought something

tragic had Happen and when you saw the

Concerned and expression on my face You Said

don't be afraid it's nothing bad or sad. Then you

proceeded to explain To me all about the important

things in life, for example love, friendship, marriage,

Finances, AND relationships with others in life etc.

From that day hence forth I knew I could

Come to you and tell you anything.

Thanks for being my confidant.

I LOVE YOU

Generous Love

I often wondered how you had so

Much Love for everyone, no

matter who they were, you

showed and gave Love

Generously, All the kids in the neighborhood

Call you Mom. When I asked you why they call

You Mom you said, because it takes a village

to raise a kid. I didn't understand what she

was talking About at the time, but later on

in life it Became perfectly clear what

she had said.

Happy Mother's Day to all

MOTHERS IN THE HOOD

I LOVE YOU

MANAGING MONEY

You did the best you could with what you had.

You manage, and budget the small Pay check

right down to the nickel. You never once complained

about the Amount of money you made. You always said,

to all of us," A little job is better than no job at all.

"We couldn't afford the designer shoes, and clothes

Those other kids were wearing in the neighborhood.

The other kids in neighborhood would tease

and make fun us. Those lessons of spending wisely

also prepared us to understand family values and

love, Happy Mother's Day.

A penny save is a penny earn.

Cash is King and Credit is Queen

I LOVE YOU

MOTHER'S CLICHÉ'S

The two most important things

My Mother taught me were.

1. It's not what you say, but how
   You say it.
2. It's not what you do, but how
   You do it.

Happy Mother's Day

Happy Mother's Day

Happy Mother's Day

Happy Mother's Day

I LOVE YOU

SEED SOWING

Mom, you said there are

Three important things in

Life, love of family, belief in one's self

And the belief in your supreme being (God).

You said, if you sow a seed in all

three, then life will be good to you.

I have since found out you were

Right.

Happy Mother's day

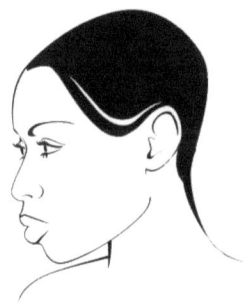

I LOVE YOU

☺A HAPPY FACE

In all the years I have

known you, You never had

a sad face, a tired look, an

angry expression or utter

words that lack faith.

But you have always

Presented yourself like a

Single rose in a garden of weeds

Symbolizing Love, hope, and peace.

I LOVE YOU

MOTHERERLY TRAITS

You were strict like a drill

Sergeant in the Army.

You discipline like a teacher in a

School.

You set guidelines like a man.

You made sure we adhered to

Rules like a father.

And you were gentle like a woman.

For you are a Mother.

HAPPY MOTHER'S DAY

I LOVE YOU

MISTAKES

When it happened and I found out, I thought maybe

I should try and hide it from her or better yet do something

unthinkable, which would affect me

for the rest of my life.

When I told you, you just smile and said, "we will

be loving and go on with our lives, and make the best of it"

For those who have not made a

mistake let them cast the first stone.

Thanks mom for being so loving and

understanding.

I LOVE YOU

HALL OF FAME

Being a single parent you wore many

hats and never once complained.

You were family counselor, financial

planner, nurse, and doctor.
But the importance role of mother,
you did so well, you should be
inducted in the Mother's hall of fame.
And if there were such an award I
would gladly, award it to you
And upon presenting it to you,
I would say,

"I thank God that he chose you to be
my Mother."

I LOVE YOU.

HAPPINESS IN LIFE

As the years past in

life, there comes a time

when you realize all the

wonderful things your

Mother did to make you

happy. Thanks Mom for

making me happy and

showing me what real

happiness is in life.

I LOVE YOU.

TEACHER

If THERE'S ONE Title I would

Bestow upon you (Mother) it would

Be teacher. For you taught

Me to trust, love, and to

Respect others. You taught

Me not to be judgmental, And to not

stereotype. You Taught me not to look

at a Person's race, color, religion, Creed,

gender, or sexual preferences, But the

content of a person

Character.

HAPPY MOTHER'S DAY

I LOVE YOU

MOTHER'S FAMOUS QUOTES

The things I remember most

about my Mother was the

things she said repeatedly like.

It's not what you are wearing, it is how you are wearing it.
You are the company that you keep.
Always keep a smile on your face and the truth shall set you free.

Happy Mother's Day

I LOVE YOU.

COMMITMENT

Mom you taught me that commitment is so much apart of love, that it should be taught in the schools, at home and in church. For you said, you have to be committed to one's self in order to receive, give and be loved.

Happy Mother's Day.

I LOVE YOU

THE VALUE OF EDUCATION

I don't remember all the things you said but I do remember one of the most important things you said, "you need a good education so you can have a good life, because people can take everything you own, but they can never take away what you have learned," and you were right a college education is so important in life,

B.A. B.S. M.A. M.S. and Ph. D.

TODAYS'S MOTHERS

Being a Mother in this

complex society is not an

easy task.

But to my Mother who

devoted her life to raising us.

May she be blessed today,

tomorrow, and forever.

Happy Mother's Day

I LOVE YOU.

NO BAD HABITS

You didn't do drugs.

You didn't smoke cigarettes.

You didn't even drink alcohol,

You didn't use profanity.

You said always strive to do the

right thing.

God bless you on this day.

And now that I am a mother, I

want to be just like you.

Happy Mother's Day

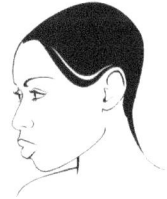

I LOVE YOU.

MOTHER'S TEN GOLDEN RULES

1. Do unto others as you would Want them to do unto you.
2. You can run but you can't hide.
3. Have Faith in your God and Yourself.
4. Don't lie to others.
5. Be honest in life.
6. Love your fellow man and Neighbors.
7. Save for a rainy day.
8. Don't binge drink alcohol; say no to drugs and smoking cigarettes.
9. Treat a woman with respect.
10. Get a college education and a vocational Trade. To all Mothers that have taught their kids the ten gold rules, you are truly Mothers of earth.

PS. No texting while driving, JW

I LOVE YOU

HONESTY AND LOVE

The other day I was in the mall shopping, when I found this woman's wallet, and returned it to her.

I am so glad I learned from you that honesty is still the best policy. For you once said, "that if you are honest, trusting, caring, then you are loving".

I LOVE YOU

TALKED ABOUT

As a beautiful women in your younger days. People talk about your grace. People talk about your beauty. People talk about your poise and people talk about your intelligence. But what people don't talk about is your motherly know how. Thank God because if they did they would be talking about you forever.
Happy Mother's Day Mom.

I LOVE YOU.

QUESTIONS IN LIFE

Is a person strong because they

Have strength?

Is a person influential because

They have persuasive powers?

Is a person intelligent because

They have a formal college

Degree?

Is a person a good Mother

Because they have children?

Thanks Mom for the

Provocative questions in life.

I LOVE YOU.

WISDOM OF MONEY

Mom, you said money is

Not answer to everything in

Life, and that it is only part

Of life big puzzle.

You said that money can't

Buy *love* and *happiness* and

It's how you use money that

Makes a difference in life.

Thanks for that lesson on

Money, and teaching me the

Wisdom of money.

Pay yourself first, others second,

and tithe to the church.

I LOVE YOU

HER PRESENCE

As she stood in the kitchen

I could feel her energy,

As she stood in the family

Room I could hear her

Laughter. As she stood over

Me at night and gave me a

Good night kiss

On my cheek

I could feel her love,

Love,

Love,

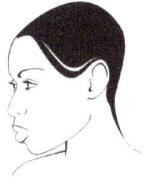

I LOVE YOU MOM

BEING THERE

You were there like the

Moon during the night.

You were there like the stars

That guides us at night.

You were there like the sun

That gave us the day light.

You were there no matter

What to make us feel love,

Safe, secure, and wanted in every

Way.

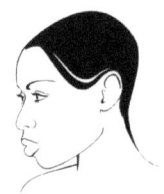

I LOVE YOU.

LIFE

To my Mother on this day I would like to thank you for giving me life. Life to know right from wrong. Life to be loving and kind instead of hate and animosity. Life to know justice from injustice, but most importantly teaching me how to live life.

I LOVE YOU.

MANNERISM

You greeted the world with simplicity. Yet you stood out above the rest. It wasn't what you wore that mattered, but how you was wearing it. It weren't the words you spoke. but how you spoke them, for you have shown me that you don't have to be the best dress or most outspoken to be notice and heard.

Happy Mother's Day

I LOVE YOU.

MANY FACETS

OF LOVE

You have shown me that

Love is an abundance of

Things, love can be just

Listening to someone's

Problem, love can be just

Being there when someone

Needs comforting, love can be just

A simple "hello" that brings

A smile to a stranger's face.

I LOVE YOU

GREATEST MOM

I can't remember my

Age when it happen to

Me.

I can't remember the

Place where it happen to

Me, but I do remembered

Saying the words,

"You are the greatest

Mom of them all."

Happy Mother's Day

I LOVE YOU

MAKING A

DIFFERENCE

People may say many things about you, but they never can say terrible things about you. for with the goodness of your heart, you cared for the world. You exemplified the saying, "one person can make a difference."

I LOVE YOU

BLESSING THE FOOD

Sometimes I would look in the
Refrigerator and see that there
Was very little food in it. But
Come dinner time a miracle
Would take place when we sat at
The dining room table, there
would be an abundance of food
on the table. It reminded me of
Jesus feeding the multitude with
just one fish. You showed me it's
not how much you have but how
you bless and serve it.

I LOVE YOU.

THROUGH MY EYES

I have met many people

In my life but none have

Shown me the courage, the

Wisdom, the understanding,

And the character, that you

Have shown the world

Through my eyes.

Happy Mother's Day.

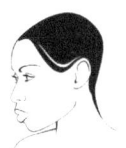

I LOVE YOU

AWAYS PRAISING

You never once took me for

Granted. You never once

Said I was, "stupid, too fat,

Or no good for nothing."

You always offered words

Of encouragement even in

Times of despair and low

Self-esteem.

Happy Mother's Day

I LOVE YOU

Cuddling arms

The merry go round was lots of

Fun to me. The playground

Brought lots of laughter to me.

But nothing brought more

Warmth to my heart, then to be Cuddled in

your arms and to Hear you say, "I Love you"

So on this day I want to cuddle You in

my arms and return the

Warmth and say,

"I LOVE YOU"

RIGHT AND WRONG

You didn't believed in

Punishing us and you

Didn't believe in beating us.

When we did something

Wrong you took us to the

Side and explained to us,

What we did wrong, then

Showed us what we did

Wrong, then you talked

about how to do it right,

the next time.

I LOVE YOU.

HONOR THY MOTHER

Although I am sending you

Flowers and gifts on this

Day. You taught me to

Honor and love you every

Day as the bible states in

The ten commandments.

For being a mother is not

Just one day, but 27/8, 365 days a year,

every day. Mom I truly love you every

day of my life.

Happy mother's Day

I LOVE YOU.

Love a Noun

Mother, what makes the

Words I love you so

Profound, is the word Love

A Noun is in between two

Pronouns, I and you.

A noun is stronger than a

Pronoun, but all are needed

to say.

I LOVE YOU

Happy Mother's Day

LOVE'S INVISIBLE SHIELD

You would shield me from

The fierce winds

You would shield me from

A burning fire.

You would shield me from an

Oncoming car.

I am not just saying this for

I know this to be true because SHE did it for

others I know SHE Would do it for me.

I LOVE YOU MOMMY.

THE ROSE

The rose has come to

Symbolize love. Before I

Knew a rose symbolized

Love, you were there. Before I Could walk

or talk you were

there. Before I knew I was

being born you was there.

Now that I am grown you

Are still there. So today I am

giving you a rose for every year you

were there, to share your life and

love with me.

I LOVE YOU.

THE EFFECTS OF LOVE

Mom, whenever we were

Together you made me

forget all of my worries,

troubles, trials, and tribulations,

for you're the type of

Person that has that effect

On everyone.

For time appears to stand

Still whenever we are

Together.

Happy Mother's Day.

I LOVE YOU.

LOVE

(A PRECIOUS AWARD)

For all the awards I've

Received in my life, the

Award that is dearest to my

Heart, is the award of love

That a mother and child have

between them. It's an award

that can't be bought or sold

and is never, ever for sale.

Happy Mother's Day

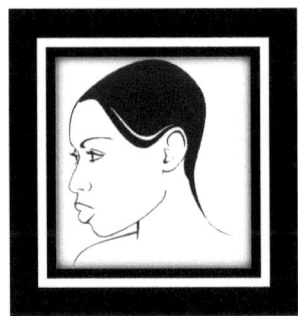

Holiday and Days

Although the seasons come

And go, and the different

Holidays only come once a

Year, you were there every

Morning to make my day

Sunny and bright. You were

There to make every rainy

Day a sunny day delight.

Happy mother's Day

I LOVE YOU

Mother's

AUTOBIOGRAPHY

If I had written Gone

With The Wind or Titanic it

would have been a minor

achievement compared to

having you as my mother.

For your life story of love,

For one's family would endure

forever.

Happy Mother's Day

A WEALTH OF *LOVE*

The wealth of a person

Doesn't necessarily make

Everyone happier.

But a wealth of love of one

Person can make everyone

Happy and joyful.

Happy Mother's Day

Happy Mother's Day

Happy Mother's Day

Happy Mother's Day

I LOVE YOU

GLOWING

There is a glow around you

That says you're special.

There is a glow around you

That says you are caring.

There's a glow around you

That says you are sharing

And there is a glow around

You wherever you go.

Happy Mother's Day

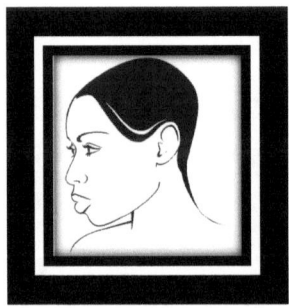

I LOVE YOU

WRONG PERCEPTION OF LOVE

Some people confuses

Kissing and hugs with

loving, these are only

affections.

Loving is a much deeper

emotion and comes from

the heart, for the heart is

the essence of our love.

Thanks Mom for giving

your heart to me.

Happy Mother's Day

I LOVE YOU

THOUGHTS THAT COUNT

Roses are red, violets are blue this poem was written especially for you. And no matter how simple it may sound, for I know "mother" you realize that it's the thoughts that count more than the Gifts that is received. Happy Mother's Day

I LOVE YOU

CONTINUOUS FLOW

OF *LOVE*

Like the Lakes that runs into

Rivers.

Like the Rivers that runs

into seas.

Likes the seas that runs into

the oceans.

Your motherly love will

forever run in me.

Happy Mother's Day

I LOVE YOU

THE NEED FOR EACH OTHER

Like a leaf that attaches to a

Branch.

Like a branch that attaches to a

tree.

Like a tree deeply rooted into

the ground.

Your love will remain deeply

rooted in me. For without the leaves

the branches cannot stand, and without

the branches the trees will surely

Perish.

I LOVE YOU.

THE JOURNEY OF LIFE

If the journey of a thousand miles begin with one step, Then the journey of a life begins with one's mother,

Conception,

First Trimester,

Second Trimester,

Third Trimester,

Birth.

Happy Mother's Day

I LOVE YOU

DESCRIPTION OF A

MOTHER

Her voice is as lovely as

humming birds singing.

Her walking is as graceful

as a ballerina performing

on stage.

Her skin is as soft as a silk scarf,

Yet she is the most humble

woman I ever known.

A perfect description of a

Mother.

I LOVE YOU

FORGIVENESS OF A _MOTHER_

I tried psychological manipulation on her in a funny way, but she caught on. I tried jokes on her in which some of them were not funny nor amusing. I ran away from home for two days and I'm sure she was worried about me. But no matter what I did, she always welcome me back with open arms, a hug and a kiss. For she was always a loving and forgiving Mother.

I LOVE YOU.

INGREDIENTS OF LOVE

Love is something that can't

be taught in schools but

must be shown and

express at home. For Love is

a mixture of many

ingredients, Touching,

hugging, sharing, and caring,

etc.

Thanks Mom for giving me

all the ingredients.

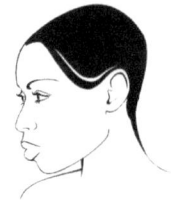

I LOVE YOU

MANSION

We didn't live in a mansion. But if you were visiting our home you would swear that we lived in one because of all the hospitality that radiates from mother. She was always smiling, happy, cheerful, and so much fun to be with.
Happy Mother's Day

I LOVE YOU

NICKNAMES

My friends nicknamed my Mother, "Cookie," because every time one of my friends came over she would always offer them some cookies and a glass of milk, surprisingly no one ever refused her.

Happy Mother's Day

"Cookie"

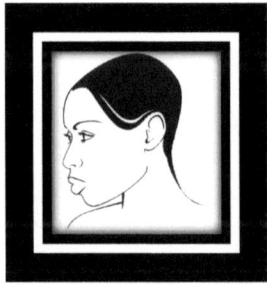

I LOVE YOU

DIFFERENT LANGUAGES

I wish I could say "I love you" Mother in every Language on earth. But I can't so I'll just say it in English, Spanish, French, German, and Italian. For it doesn't matter what language you say it in it still means the same.

Te amo.

Des je t'aime

Ich liebe dich

I LOVE YOU

INTUITIVE POWERS

You knew what was wrong

before I open my Mouth.

You felt my pain before I

said, "ouch." You gave me

your smile when I was sad

and depressed.

Thank God for Mother's

intuitive powers

Happy Mother's Day

I LOVE YOU

TWINS

We were not twins but

when you hurt, I hurt.

when I cry, you cried. When I

needed comforting, you

were comforting.

When you are happy, I'm

happy. No we are not twins, but

our DNA is so close we

could be twins, but we are

just family.

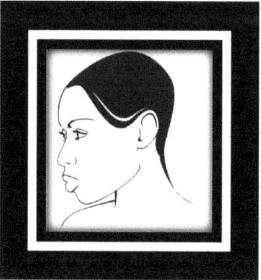

I LOVE YOU

FAITH

Lost in the forest struggling against mother nature in a snow storm for days. I found inner strength from from the memories of my natural mother's saying to me as a child such as, "you can overcome anything if you have "Faith." Faith it's such a powerful word I wish I could give it to everyone as you have given it to me.

I LOVE YOU

MIRACLES

When I received the sad

news I text you about

it. You said in your text

"everything will be alright,"

if I just trust in the man

above. Six months later

the Doctor told me I was

in remission. It was your

belief, prayer, caring, and

support that made a difference.

Miracles still happens

Everyday.

I LOVE YOU

SAY IT WITH LOVE

I have written about twenty

poem to express the way I

feel about you at this

particular moment in my

life. Finally I realized it's not

the way I use the words or

the ways in which I say the words, as

long as I say them with

LOVE.

I LOVE YOU

TOUCHED BY AN

ANGEL

Words can't express how I feel in

my heart about you, mother.

Even the words I love you can't

come close to what I feel.

If I had one wish, it would be

that an angel would come down

from heaven and take this feeling

I have and touch you with it.

That is the only way I can

describe how much love I have for you

from the bottom of my heart and soul.

I LOVE YOU

CHANGE

A person is wise when they accept change. They are even wiser when they are prepared for change. For surely change will come as the season themselves shall come and go.

Happy Mother's Day

I LOVE YOU

SAINT

As I look back you gave

me strength when I was

weak.

You gave me hope when I

was in despair.

You gave me light when it Was

dark. You were my earthly saint

when I needed you most.

Happy Mother's Day

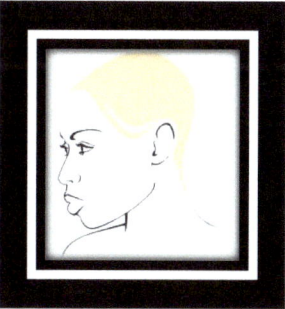

I LOVE YOU

WORRYING

Your face never showed any worried lines. For you always said, "don't worry because what will happen, will happen."
You said, "if you have a problem try to solve it but don't worry about it" for it won't go away with worrying. Now I know why your face doesn't have any worried lines, and is so beautiful.

I LOVE YOU

TIMELESS COMMITMENT OF LOVE

One of the most wonderful

commitment between a

mother and child is the love

they share together.

That commitment of love

between mother and child is

a commitment for life.

It is a commitment not only

for good times, but for all

time.

I LOVE YOU

LOVE

Love is the small component

of friendship.

Love is the main ingredient

for marriage.

Love and patience is

required to be a good mother.

Happy Mother's Day

I LOVE YOU

LOVE IS GIVEN

FREELY

You have to earn a P.H.D from college. You have to earn respect from others. But love is something that is never earned, but is given freely with no cost to others.

Happy Mother's Day

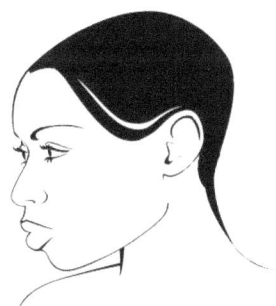

I LOVE YOU

IMMEASURABLE LOVE

The love of a Mother is

higher than the highest

mountain.

The love of a Mother is

deeper than the deepest sea.

The love of a Mother is

stronger than the strongest

metal. The love of a mother is not

just for a moment in time

but is timeless.

I LOVE YOU

TRUE MEANING OF

LOVE

Love is never having to say

you're sorry.

Love is never having to

apologize.

Love is never having to

explain your actions for

love is always loving.

I LOVE YOU

HAPPINESS

Happiness is helping other

realize their DREAMS.

Happiness is helping others

achieved their GOALS.

Happiness is showing

others how to enjoy

their success.

Happy Mother's Day

I LOVE YOU

LOVE

(Internally and Eternally)

Friendship is a promise of

love.

Marriage is a commitment of

Love.

Motherly Love is an

internal and eternal

Love.

Happy Mother's Day

I LOVE YOU

A MILLION TIMES

I CAN SAY

I LOVE YOU

I LOVE YOU

I LOVE YOU

I LOVE YOU

I LOVE YOU

I LOVE YOU

I LOVE YOU

I LOVE YOU

I can say it a million

times and still not say it

enough.

I LOVE YOU

100

The following books are available

through

The Publisher, Checkmate Inc.

at www.checkmate1776.com

"50 Ways to Say I Love You"

to help celebrate a Birthday,

Anniversaries, or Valentine's Day.

"100 Ways To Say I Love You Mother"

Allow 7-10 days for delivery. Postage,

tax, and handling included in price, but

is subject to change at the company and author

discretion, without notice to general public.

Checkmate Inc.
2970 Tall Pine Lane
Suite # 8
Jacksonville, FL 32277.
Telephone: 904-226-0536

Email: Jameswatson1492@gmail.com

www.ingramcontent.com/pod-product-compliance
Lightning Source LLC
Chambersburg PA
CBHW040926190426
43197CB00033B/106